The Economics of Energy

The Pros and Cons of Offshore Drilling

Alison Gaines

Cavendish Square
New York

Published in 2016 by Cavendish Square Publishing, LLC
243 5th Avenue, Suite 136, New York, NY 10016

Website: cavendishsq.com

This publication represents the opinions and views of the author based on his or her personal experience, knowledge, and research. The information in this book serves as a general guide only. The author and publisher have used their best efforts in preparing this book and disclaim liability rising directly or indirectly from the use and application of this book.

CPSIA Compliance Information: Batch #CW16CSQ

All websites were available and accurate when this book was sent to press.

Library of Congress Cataloging-in-Publication Data

Gaines, Alison.
The pros and cons of offshore drilling / Alison Gaines.
pages cm. — (The economics of energy)
Includes bibliographical references and index.
ISBN 978-1-5026-0960-1 (hardcover) ISBN 978-1-5026-0961-8 (ebook)
1. Offshore oil well drilling. 2. Fossil fuels. I. Title.

TN871.3.G34 2016
333.8'2309162—dc23

2015032452

Editorial Director: David McNamara
Editor: Amy Hayes/Ryan Nagelhout
Copy Editor: Nathan Heidelberger
Art Director: Jeffrey Talbot

Designer: Amy Greenan
Production Manager: Jennifer Ryder-Talbot
Production Editor: Renni Johnson
Photo Researcher: J8 Media

The Economics of Energy

Table of Contents

5   Chapter 1
Oil, Our Favorite Fossil Fuel

23   Chapter 2
The Pros of Offshore Drilling

41   Chapter 3
The Cons of Offshore Drilling

59   Chapter 4
Deeper and Deeper

73   Glossary

76   Find Out More

78   Index

80   About the Author

A modern-day offshore drilling platform. In shallower water (shallower than 3,000 feet, or 914 meters), the platform stands on legs that extend all the way down to the ocean floor. There are other types of platforms for deeper water, such as floating structures.

Chapter 1

Oil, Our Favorite Fossil Fuel

It might not be an exaggeration to say that the modern world is addicted to oil. Oil is used for so many things: not just for fuel but also for the asphalt in the road on which we drive. It is not just used to lubricate machine parts, but it is also an ingredient in the actual items we manufacture, from shoes to clothes to toothbrushes to shampoo.

Oil is a **fossil fuel**. Coal and natural gas are also fossil fuels. They are resources that we burn for energy and are made of the remains of organisms that were at one time alive, now embedded beneath the Earth's surface, hence the use of the word "fossil." In the case of oil, these fossils have turned into a liquid deep beneath the Earth's surface. It is estimated by the International Energy Agency that in 2010, fossil fuels provided for 71.4 percent of the world's energy use. The most consumed fossil fuel worldwide is, by far, oil.

Today, the main way that we access **crude oil**, or **petroleum**, is by drilling for it in undersea **wells** in the oceans. It is a multi-billion-dollar industry, and it has created the need for new technology. Many of the important advances in technology we owe to oil.

Most of Earth's resources are not infinite, and oil is no exception. We are using up oil much faster than Earth produces it, and one day there

A DEEPER DIVE

How Does the Earth Make Oil?

According to the most widely accepted theory today, the oil and natural gas now pumped out of the ground come from dead plants and animals from millions of years ago—286 to 360 million years ago, to be exact. At that time, the oceans were full of life-forms, many of them microscopic. When these creatures died, they eventually became part of the mud, clay, and silt in the ground. Layers and layers of this material formed over the years, and the layers eventually turned into sedimentary rock. Sandstone, shale, and dolomite are types of sedimentary rock made from this process.

As the materials decayed and experienced heat and pressure from being in the Earth, they transformed into oil and gas. When oil is found, it is usually beneath layers of sedimentary rock, along with pockets of gas (which is lighter than oil) and water (which is heavier).

How petroleum is made: organic life dies and returns to the ground (*left*). It becomes sedimentary rock (*center*), and as it gets closer to the center of the Earth, the pressure turns it into oil and gas (*right*).

This is known as the organic theory of the origin of oil and gas. According to this theory, petroleum is created over time by the decomposition of organic matter, but at a very slow rate, much slower than it is being drilled today.

Petroleum is the technical name for this oil found beneath Earth's surface, which is made over millions of years. Petroleum is a liquid mixture of hydrocarbons, which are organic compounds containing carbon (which is contained in all life) and hydrogen.

will be none left. **Offshore drilling** allows oil to be extracted at a faster rate than ever before. Because of this, the world may run out of oil more quickly. So, many people are questioning whether the energy industry should continue to rely on it so heavily.

How Did We Start Using Oil in the First Place?

Before people began drilling for oil, they were drilling for salt. In North America, settlers heading west used salt to preserve food, particularly meat, which they could take on their journey. Hand-drilled wells produced **brine**, which when boiled off, left salt. Sometimes, crude oil would emerge from these wells, too, and people often considered this "rock oil" useless. It was far from useless—they just didn't know it yet.

Looking for Light

Along with salt, people needed light. In the mid-1800s, reading and writing were catching on as leisure activities. However, most people still made a living by farming. Since they farmed during the day, they often only had time to read at night, and they needed light for this. Factories also needed more light so they could operate during the shorter days of winter. People had used tallow candles and whale oil for light, but those sources were becoming costly and, in the case of whale oil, harder to find. Early attempts to distill crude oil into lamp fuel were not perfect—the result smelled bad and made lots of smoke. However, it became wildly popular once oil was more widely available and distillation methods improved.

The First Wells

In 1858, James Miller Williams, a carriage maker from New Jesey living in Hamilton, Canada, was the first to successfully drill for oil in North America. He did so in an area now called Oil Springs. (History often awards this credit to Edwin Drake, an American, but in truth, Williams struck oil a year before Drake did.) Crude oil was often found on Earth's surface as part of "gum beds," or tar-like pits, along with asphalt-like material that people often harvested for various uses, such as sealant for canoes. Williams believed that he could find more crude oil beneath these gum beds, and he was right. Over one hundred wells were soon drilled in Oil Springs, and it was not long before drilling started across the border in the United States as well.

The first person to drill for oil in the United States was Edwin Drake, a retired railroad conductor. Under a contract from the newly formed Seneca Oil Company, Drake investigated places to drill near Titusville, Pennsylvania, close to the brine wells.

Drake became successful because he invented the drivepipe. The first drivepipe was a cast-iron pipe made of three 10-foot (3-meter) joints. Drake pushed the pipe into the ground until he hit bedrock 32 feet (9.8 m) under. Then, he lowered the drilling tools through the pipe. The pipe made it so that the drilling hole wouldn't collapse on the tools due to water damage. This principle is still used in many kinds of drilling today.

Drake struck oil in August in 1859. People were so excited to have found a way to access oil that they paid $20 per **barrel**, a very high price at the time.

At the time of Williams's and Drake's drilling discoveries, people only needed oil to lubricate machine parts and to light lamps. But a few years later, the American Civil War began, and it became clear that oil was very

A DEEPER DIVE

Kerosene Lights Up the Night

The lamp fuel that ended up catching on was called kerosene. Abraham Gesner, a chemist and geologist from Nova Scotia, Canada, was the first in North America to distill a hydrocarbon into lamp fuel. He called the product kerosene, a mix of the Greek words for "oil" and "wax." In 1853, he moved his operation to Long Island, New York, and built one of the world's first refineries, where the raw materials were made into usable lamp oil. At first, Gesner mostly made kerosene out of coal oil. However, he also could make it from petroleum. When petroleum became readily available through drilling, and once people soon figured out how to refine it, kerosene refined from petroleum became the go-to lamp fuel, until electricity came along.

Before Thomas Edison invented the light bulb in 1879, people relied on kerosene as an accessible and affordable lighting option.

Edwin Drake (*right*) in front of his well in Titusville, Pennsylvania.

valuable. The many factories that were making steam engines, cannons, firearms, clothing, and other necessary war items all needed lubrication for their machines and light to work through the night.

Drilling has since spread across the United States, and oil has become a staple of life nearly everywhere. People wanted oil so much that they eventually followed it into the ocean.

Modern Petroleum Uses

Oil is the main ingredient in most transportation fuels used today. Oil companies make different types of fuel, each appropriate for a different kind of engine. It is estimated that every day it takes about 30 million barrels of oil (one barrel is 42 gallons or 159 liters) to fuel the entire world's cars, trucks, trains, ships, and planes.

However, our gas tanks are far from the only place we encounter petroleum in our daily lives. "**Petrochemicals**" is a broad term for all the chemical substances that are derived from crude oil at refineries and petrochemical complexes. Petrochemicals make up many of the products that we use in our daily lives, the most common being **plastic**.

Plastics are materials that can be heated and molded into a shape. They are made of long, chainlike molecules called polymers. There are many different types of plastic with different chemical makeups.

Other nonplastic resources made from petrochemicals include detergents, cleaning fluids, synthetic rubber, synthetic fibers (like polyester, acrylic, and spandex), beauty products, paints, clothing dyes, ink, foam, medicines, and paraffin wax (which is found in crayons, candles, and polishes). Some of these items are things that we used to,

Some products, such as many technological devices, cannot be made without petrochemicals. Other products, like clothes, existed before petrochemicals but are hardly made without them today.

or still can, get from natural sources. Rubber, for example, comes from a rubber plant. People have been making clothing and dyes for centuries from plant and animal sources. However, petrochemicals have made it possible to manufacture synthetic versions at a very fast rate. It may be possible to conserve fossil fuels by returning to these original sources. Even so, some of the items in this list, such as the plastic in a laptop computer, would not have been possible without oil.

The Move Offshore

In 1896, Henry L. Williams and his associates constructed a pier reaching 300 feet (91 m) out into the Pacific Ocean near Santa Barbara, California.

He mounted a **rig** to it, inventing the first offshore oil well. He essentially used the same drilling techniques that had been used on land. A year later, the well Williams helped construct was producing oil, and within the next five years, twenty-two other companies followed suit, building piers and drilling wells offshore in the Pacific Ocean. This was the beginning of offshore drilling in the United States.

In 1911, Gulf Refining Co. began drilling in Caddo Lake, Louisiana, without the use of piers connecting the offshore rigs to the land. This is

The beginnings of offshore drilling consisted of piers attached to the shore. These are the wells in the Summerland oil fields of Santa Barbara, California, near the end of the 1800s.

A Timeline of Offshore Drilling

1854 George Bissell forms the Pennsylvania Rock Oil Company of New York; the name is later changed to Seneca Oil

1858 James Miller Williams strikes oil in Ontario, Canada

1859 Edwin L. Drake strikes oil in Pennsylvania on August 27

1896 Henry L. Williams constructs a pier reaching 300 feet (91 m) out into the Pacific Ocean off the beach near Santa Barbara, California; this is often regarded as the first instance of offshore drilling

1911 Gulf Refining Co. constructs first true offshore rig in Caddo Lake, Louisiana

1945 President Harry Truman proclaims that the federal government is in charge of the whole continental shelf; individual states want this control, and so begins the Tidelands Dispute

1947 Kerr-McGee builds the first oil-producing rig out of sight of land; the Kermac No. 16 well stood in about 18 feet (5.5 m) of water, 10 miles (16 km) offshore, in the Gulf of Mexico

1953 President Dwight D. Eisenhower passes the Submerged Lands Act; later that same year, he passes the Outer Continental Shelf Lands Act

1969 Santa Barbara blowout occurs on January 28

1973–1974 In response to the United States' aid of Israel, the Organization of the Petroleum Exporting Countries (OPEC) institutes an oil embargo against the United States; production is still low from the Santa Barbara blowout a few years earlier, creating an energy crisis in the United States

1975 The first discovery of oil deeper than 1,000 feet (305 m) is made in Shell's Cognac field in the Gulf of Mexico; Shell drills 1,025 feet (312.4 m), the deepest offshore discovery yet

1984 Conoco uses the first tension-leg platform to drill in the North Sea

1989 *Exxon Valdez* tanker hits a reef in Prince William Sound, Alaska, on March 24

2010 BP's Macondo well in the Gulf of Mexico blows out on April 20 and is not capped until June 4, the largest oil spill in US history

2015 Despite great protests from environmentalists, President Barack Obama allows conditional approval for Shell to drill for oil and gas in the Arctic Ocean

more abundant oil in deeper water. In drilling language, "**deepwater**" is water deeper than 1,000 feet (305 m). In 1975, Shell Oil Company made the first deepwater oil discovery in the Gulf of Mexico at 1,025 feet (312.4 m) deep.

Geologists discovered that the ocean's deepwater areas were easier to penetrate than ground in shallower waters. Also, the wells yielded much more oil. Shallow water wells usually produced a few thousand barrels per day. The deepwater wells, however, regularly exceeded 10,000 barrels per day (420,000 gal, or 1.6 million L). As soon as it became clear that deepwater drilling was extremely lucrative, companies raced to find these rich areas.

Offshore drilling began to replace onshore drilling with more and more deepwater discoveries. Between 1991 and 2002, each year was more productive than the last, and by 2002, offshore **oil production** yielded more than 2 million barrels per day (98 million gal, or 318 million L). By the end of the 1990s, deepwater production had surpassed shallow water production, with an increasing amount coming from ultra-deepwater discoveries deeper than 5,000 feet (1524 m).

CRITICAL THINKING

- Think of a few objects you use every single day, objects you couldn't live without. How many of these do you think are made from petroleum? (Hint: most plastics are made from petroleum.) Do you think our society is dependent on petroleum? Do you depend on it?

- Why are there restrictions on where offshore drilling may take place?

- How do you think the world would have developed differently if oil drilling had not been discovered?

Working on an offshore rig is taxing and usually involves living away from land for weeks at a time.

Chapter 2

The Pros of Offshore Drilling

Drilling a well involves making a hole thousands of feet deep in the Earth's surface. As they go, the drillers line the hole with a steel pipe and pour cement around it. The steel and cement are meant to keep the drilling hole in place and to keep the oil from moving upward around or through the pipe. Then, when or if they reach oil, the drillers have to keep the oil from escaping the well at enormous pressure. The process is often compared to popping the cork on a bottle—if the bottle were full of hot petroleum that wants to escape at as much as 18,000 pounds of pressure per square inch (124 million pascals).

Because the well is so deep underwater, the subsea work cannot be done by hand, so all of this is done using underwater robotic technology. On board the rig, people are working twenty-four hours a day—controlling the subsea electronics, fixing and maintaining the heavy machinery above water, making sure the engines are working ... Managing a deep-sea oil rig takes many people, usually working in twelve- or fourteen-hour shifts around the clock, to make sure that everything is operating at the correct pressures and that the oil is flowing properly.

A DEEPER DIVE

What Is OPEC?

The phenomenon of cartelization can be seen in the Organization of the Petroleum Exporting Countries, or OPEC. Today it is made up of twelve member countries: Algeria, Angola, Ecuador, Iran, Iraq, Kuwait, Libya, Nigeria, Qatar, Saudi Arabia, the United Arab Emirates, and Venezuela. Ironically, OPEC was formed in 1960 due to fears that the major oil companies were controlling prices. Now it sets production targets for its member nations. By controlling how much oil is produced in these twelve countries, OPEC plays a large part in controlling the price of oil around the world.

An example of how cartelization works: OPEC usually meets twice a year and makes its decisions by voting. Each country gets one vote, and in order for a decision to be made, the result of the vote has to be unanimous. At its November 2014 meeting, there was an oversupply of oil in OPEC nations, and crude prices had been on the downswing for several months. Several of the countries within OPEC asked for the supply target to be lowered so that prices might rise again. However, OPEC decided

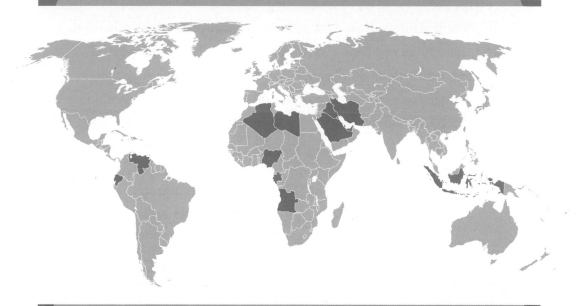

The countries shaded green are members of OPEC, the Organization of Petroleum Exporting Countries. Nations shaded orange are former OPEC members.

not to restrict supply at that point, so oil prices remained low, dipping below $50 per barrel in January 2015. As a result of the continued relatively low prices, many oil producers around the world have had to cut back on costly operations. These producers shut down operations when they won't make enough money to cover the costs.

Low oil prices might mean good things for the average consumer, but oil-exporting governments and oil companies make a lot less money when oil is cheaper. Depending on whom you talk to, low oil prices can be a good thing or a bad thing.

A DEEPER DIVE

Global Demand for Petroleum Products

The US Energy Information Administration (EIA) analyzes the global oil market and offers the following interesting facts about global petroleum demand. The United States is the world's third most populated country but consumes the most petroleum products. In 2013, it consumed nearly 19 million barrels per day (798 million gal, or 3 billion L) of refined petroleum products. Canada consumed about 2.4 million barrels per day (100.8 million gal, or 381.6 million L) that same year. China, which is the world's most populous country, has four times more people than the United States does but consumed far less oil: 10.4 million barrels per day (436.8 million gal, or 1.65 billion L).

The International Energy Agency (IEA) analyzes world oil supply and demand every quarter. For the first quarter of 2015, it showed worldwide demand at 93.12 million barrels per day (3.9 billion gal, or 14.8 billion L), and worldwide supply at 95.07 million barrels per day (4 billion gal, or 15.1 billion L). The IEA shows an increase over the past few years: as one might expect, demand and supply are increasing together. More people want to buy oil, so more people work to provide it for them.

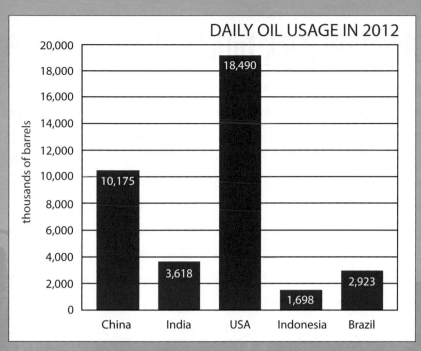

DAILY OIL USAGE IN 2012

thousands of barrels

China	10,175
India	3,618
USA	18,490
Indonesia	1,698
Brazil	2,923

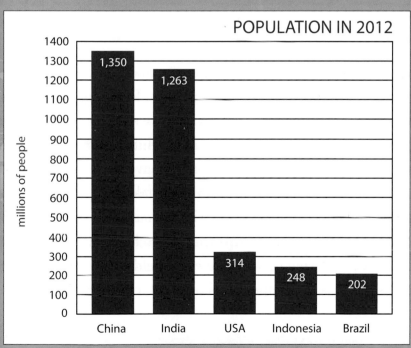

POPULATION IN 2012

millions of people

China	1,350
India	1,263
USA	314
Indonesia	248
Brazil	202

A DEEPER DIVE

Rigs to Reefs?

The undersea structures of oil platforms tend to attract marine life and become artificial reefs. Small life-forms that need hard surfaces to complete their life cycle, such as corals, barnacles, sponges, clams, bryozoans, and hydroids, start to make a home on the wooden or steel structures. This proliferation of life is a boost for animals higher up on the food chain, including larger fish and sharks. One study by Louisiana State University's Sea Grant College program found that surrounding oil platforms there is fifty times more marine life than in the surrounding mud bottoms.

The Texas Parks and Wildlife Department has its own rigs-to-reefs program, in which retired rigs are recycled to become artificial reefs. If the offshore company agrees, a crane barge lifts the above-sea portion of the rig away so that it can be recycled on land. The platform base is then dislodged from the ocean floor with explosives and carried away, then laid on its side in a designated reef site. Other times, only part of the platform base is removed, as many life-forms are already growing on it, and the top part is laid on its side next to the part still standing.

Texas is proud of its rigs-to-reef program because it allows reef activity to flourish in an area that does not

Part of a retired structure that is now a home for marine life. Artificial reefs are one reason that some argue that drilling is not harmful to the environment.

naturally create coral reefs. Temperatures in the Gulf of Mexico are often too cold, the water too murky, and the seafloor too soft for reefs to form naturally. Artificial reefs have helped some species come back from disasters such as Hurricane Katrina and the *Deepwater Horizon* blowout, and they have helped some fish recover from overfishing in the area. There are economic advantages as well: the diving and fishing industries benefit from these artificial reefs.

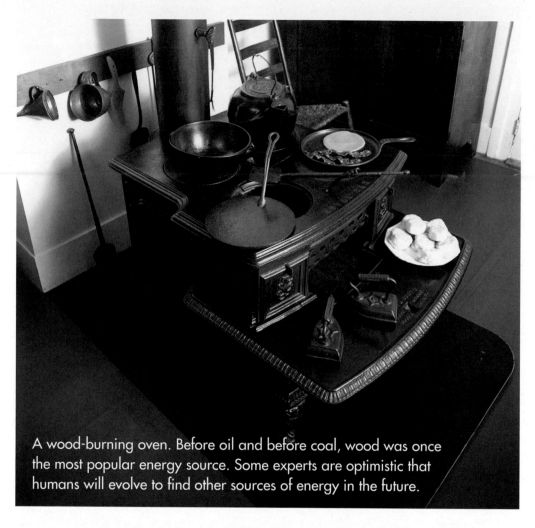

A wood-burning oven. Before oil and before coal, wood was once the most popular energy source. Some experts are optimistic that humans will evolve to find other sources of energy in the future.

"Humanity burned wood for thousands of years before arriving at coal, burned coal for about three hundred years before developing oil, and burned oil about seventy years before inventing nuclear fission," writes Simon. Depriving ourselves of oil in the present, he believes, will only make it harder and more expensive to make these future discoveries that will supply energy for centuries to come.

CRITICAL THINKING

- Read the "What is OPEC?" sidebar. When oil prices are plummeting, do you think it is OPEC's responsibility to control prices by tightening supply, or do you think the market should be left to correct itself?

- Why do people believe that more offshore drilling would lead to lower oil prices? How could lower oil prices be a good thing? A bad thing? Do you think that lower oil prices are a sufficient reason to continue drilling?

- What changes in the standard of living would you expect to see if this society suddenly had to cut down on its petroleum use?

- How could using oil in the present enable future discovery and development of other energy sources?

The edge of the oil slick of the *Deepwater Horizon* blowout in the Gulf of Mexico

Chapter 3

The Cons of Offshore Drilling

On January 28, 1969, an oil spill happened off the coast of Santa Barbara, California, that at the time was the largest the country had ever seen. Six miles (9.7 km) off the coast, a well drilled by Union Oil Company suffered a blowout, which happens when the well built by the drilling company cannot contain the pressure of the oil under the surface. Oil spurted out of the well for eleven days, releasing a total of 80,000 barrels of oil (3.4 million gal, or 12.7 million L) and covering about 30 miles (48 km) of beaches with a black, gooey mess.

The Santa Barbara incident prompted the US government to consider stricter policies on offshore drilling. Months later, the Department of the Interior under President Richard Nixon updated the rules of offshore drilling, making the guidelines Eisenhower had written seventeen years earlier much stricter. For the first time, the government claimed the ability to restrict offshore drilling in areas where the environmental risk was too great. A small amount of drilling still took place off the coast of California, but as a result of the blowout and the legislation that followed, the focus of offshore drilling in the United States shifted almost exclusively to the Gulf of Mexico.

A DEEPER DIVE

Wildlife Suffers, Humans Suffer

Hurricanes have been known to cause accidents at drilling sites. During Hurricanes Katrina and Rita in 2005, the US Minerals Management Service reports, 115 oil platforms and 457 pipelines were destroyed, causing 741,000 gallons (2.8 million L) of oil to spill into the Gulf of Mexico. For a community that has to recover from the damage of a hurricane, wreckage and spilled oil from a destroyed pipeline or platform makes life even harder.

The neighborhood of Plaquemines Parish in New Orleans, Louisiana, was profiled by National Geographic reporter Tyrone Turner in 2015. This is an area that has been hit by hurricanes many times, but the worst disaster for this community was the *Deepwater Horizon* oil blowout in 2010. Since the spill, some areas of the Mississippi River have stopped producing oysters, creating big problems and unemployment for oyster fishermen, whose livelihoods depend on the oyster supply. Those who still have their jobs as oyster fishermen have to travel farther to catch less. Some have lost their jobs, not having anywhere else to go because they have been oyster fishermen their whole lives.

Oysters are one of many species that have suffered as a result of oil spills, which affect local economies as well.

"The oyster industry was the heartbeat, the soul of the Pointe à la Hache community … and that's gone," says Byron Encalade, the president of the Louisiana Oystermen Association in Pointe à la Hache. "This place [was] recession-proof. But now look at it. It's a ghost town. Those that could get out, got out. Most of us here, we have nowhere else to go."

Five years after the spill, the oyster population had not recovered. This is not something that can be rebuilt after a hurricane like houses or boats. Not only is this a shame for people who travel to New Orleans wanting to taste oysters—it has destroyed the livelihood of the people who have lived there for generations.

When oil is spilled into the water, it can spread out over great distances. The *Exxon Valdez* spill reached shorelines as distant as 600 miles (966 km) away; the BP *Deepwater Horizon* spill reached 630 miles (1,014 km) of shorelines by the time the well was capped. While the national and international media pay attention to larger oil spills of millions of gallons, the US Environmental Protection Agency (EPA) reports that about seventy spills are reported *every day* in the United States. Not all of these are a result of offshore drilling—they can be from pipelines breaking or bursting, wells malfunctioning, other equipment failing, or transport accidents (such as the *Exxon Valdez*). Oil comes out of the ground at such a high pressure that a lot of it can spill in a short time, and even a small amount of oil can spread over a huge area, especially if the spill is happening in the water, where more and more of our oil is being accessed.

Cleanup efforts following spills only remove a fraction of the oil spilled. According to the Natural Resources Defense Council (NRDC), scientists estimate that nearly 20,000 gallons of oil (75,708 L) from the *Exxon Valdez* spill remain in Alaska's Prince William Sound. Much of the oil is not on top of the water but drifting beneath the surface in large **plumes**. These large expanses of oil, miles long, are devoid of oxygen and can be fatal to fish that swim through them.

Sometimes, the cleanup measures after an oil spill inflict their own damage. Oil companies often pump chemical compounds called dispersants into the water that are meant to keep the oil from doing more damage. Dispersants break the oil up into droplets, which prevent huge plumes of oil. Unfortunately, these dispersants are also toxic, so it is questionable whether pumping these chemical dispersants into the water is a good idea. Gelling agents, which make the oil solidify, and biological

An artist's rendering of the *Deepwater Horizon* blowout. While the oil reached 630 miles (1014 km) of coastline, it's more difficult to calculate how much oil is still under the surface.

A DEEPER DIVE

Limiting Damage to Wildlife After a Spill

In the event of an oil spill, first responders need to know which populations are in the most danger from the spill, and they will do the following three things, outlined by the US EPA:

1) **Contain the spilled oil.** First, people have to try to stop the oil at the source, to make sure that as little spills as possible. This may involve controlled burns or adding dispersants to the water. Also, oil-soaked debris and animal carcasses should be taken away.

2) **Keep animals away from spilled oil.** Often, animals won't know that they shouldn't enter an oily area. To keep animals away, people try to make the area an unappealing place. Sometimes, the presence of humans cleaning up the oil is enough to keep animals away. People sometimes use recordings of predators, or other loud and unappealing noises, to scare animals and prevent them from coming near. Fish often have sensitivity to bright lights or high-frequency vibrations. Sometimes a boat or helicopter patrols the area, and this is enough to herd animals away.

Occasionally, clean animals are captured to make sure they don't become oiled. However, as the EPA says, the conditions for this need to be perfect, and this should

Since pelicans dive for their food, oil spills affect them deeply. The brown pelican population in the Gulf of Mexico suffered as a result of the *Deepwater Horizon* incident.

only be done on animals that are especially vulnerable to oil contamination. The animal would need to be captured safely and released in a predetermined, clean area.

3) **Rescue oiled animals.** We often see pictures and stories of oil-covered animals being rescued, washed, and returned to the wild, but this is a last resort. It is not guaranteed that the animal will survive capture or even survive the return to its habitat. An animal may be able to avoid capture until it is very ill, at which point it could be too late. It is difficult to track the success rate of the animals returned to the wild: today, birds that are released are banded (with a stainless steel tag around their leg, usually) or radio-marked, which makes them easier to monitor.

agents, which accelerate the rate at which the oil biodegrades, are other chemicals sometimes used, and they also affect the water.

Another way of taking care of the oil is through controlled burns. Lighting a fire on the oil in the ocean does get the oil out of the water but also releases chemicals and smoke into the air that are harmful for both humans and animals.

In terms of danger to wildlife, contamination travels up the food chain; that is, fish or other small creatures that are contaminated with oil, or that have ingested oil, will be eaten by larger animals, which will then become sick as a result. No species is immune to oil damage, but some are more vulnerable than others. Birds are especially susceptible because when they get oil on their feathers, the feathers lose their ability to keep the bird warm and waterproof. The same goes for other animals, such as sea otters and fur seals, that rely on their fur for insulation. Animals that clean themselves with their mouth, such as preening birds and otters, ingest oil from their fur or feathers. Animals' reproductive systems can also suffer, impacting not just the population at the time of the oil spill but future generations as well. Even whales and dolphins, which do not have fur, may eat contaminated fish and become sick. Also, these creatures have to surface to breathe, and may get oil or hydrocarbon vapors into their lungs when respirating.

Spill or No Spill

Even without factoring in the spills, offshore drilling is disruptive to the environment, enough that some people believe the environmental cost is greater than the benefit of having the oil. The presence of a platform, and the pipe's cables that hold it to the sea floor, are not the only ways that a

Controlled burns, such as this one in the Gulf of Mexico, are a strategy to remove oil from the water, but they inflict other environmental damage to the air in the process.

$238.7 million to political parties and candidates since 1990. Oil and gas interest groups also lobby Congress; since 1998, more than $1 billion has been spent on lobbying efforts. This happens on national and state levels.

Much of this financial power goes to political interests and not to the people, all of whom rely on oil and gas in their everyday lives. To make matters worse, the oil and gas industry gets tax breaks and subsidies from the federal government; this is money that would otherwise go to other industries and citizens.

Because of all this, many people believe that Big Oil is still very much alive and is more interested in protecting its wealth than in safe, reasonable regulations to protect citizens. Offshore drilling is making up an increasingly large percentage of this industry. Reducing dependence on offshore drilling would mean that the average person would face higher prices for many products and an adjustment in the standard of living. But according to some, this would be worth it, if it means also reducing dependence on an industry that has so much political influence and may not always have everyone's interests at heart.

CRITICAL THINKING

- What are the ways that humans work to protect the environment, especially animals, after an oil spill? What do you think are the pros and cons of human intervention?

- Why are oil spills and blowouts such disasters? What is the worst side effect of a spill? (The oil lost, the money lost, the ruined environmental landscape, the danger to animals, the danger to humans, etc.)

- What are some of the costs to humans of an oil spill?

- Is it possible that cleanup efforts can inflict additional damage to an oiled area? How so? Is it still worth the effort?

A DEEPER DIVE

Re-Refining

Oil can only be used once—that is, unless it's recycled. Usually, after engine oil is used, it is burned, but there are many companies today in the re-refining business. They take used engine oil and recycle it so that it can be used again as base stock. (Base stock is the main ingredient of an engine oil before other chemicals, known as additives, are put in to increase its performance.) Some companies are able to reuse the by-products as asphalt and fuel.

The Independent Lubricant Manufacturers' Association (ILMA) reported that re-refining has been happening in North America since the 1970s, when it first became attractive because oil prices were so high during the oil embargo.

The ILMA said that the United States accumulates about 1 billion gallons (3.8 billion L) of used oil every year, and if it re-refined all of that, it would be able to provide for one-quarter of the country's lubricant needs. Re-refining produces less greenhouse gas and allows oil to be conserved. However, it has drifted in and out of popularity,

Re-refining used engine oil uses one-third less energy than producing new crude oil, re-refining companies say.

as people are less interested in it when the price of "virgin" (not used) oil is low.

Also, it is often difficult for re-refining companies, which are much smaller than the Big Oil companies, to collect enough used oil to operate with. Nonetheless, re-refining could become one way to make Earth's oil supply last longer.

A DEEPER DIVE

Fuel Efficiency

In recent years, many advances have been made in the area of fuel efficiency, or the amount of energy that can come from a certain amount of fuel. This gives some people confidence that energy independence is on the horizon. Most vehicles have come a long way in terms of fuel efficiency: in 1975, the average car in the United States got about 15 miles to the gallon (6.4 kilometers per liter), and in 2010 it was nearly 35 miles per gallon (14.9 km/L). Some of this has to do with the increase in hybrid and electric vehicles. Both the auto and the oil industries are under lots of pressure to continue to increase fuel efficiency: the current goal, under the Clean Air Act, is to have an average fuel economy of 55 miles per gallon (23.4 km/L) by 2025. The point of this goal is to reduce both fuel consumption and the amount of greenhouse gases being released into the atmosphere, as less fuel also means fewer emissions.

The US Department of Defense is the single largest consumer of oil: it consumes 16.8 million gallons (63.6 million liters) daily. Military machinery (fighter aircraft, battle tanks, warships) is not fuel-efficient at all.

Hybrids and battery-electric cars are one way consumers conserve oil. Unfortunately, many are too expensive to become commonplace at the moment.

An Abrams battle tank uses 5 gallons (18.9 L) of gas for every 3 miles (4.8 km) traveled: that's less than 1 mile per gallon (0.4 km/L). Ironically, the military is tasked with safeguarding the supply of oil to the United States. While it is currently involved with research to decrease oil consumption, it seems that fuel efficiency was not initially one of the military's priorities.

The energy density of wind power is much less than that of fossil fuels. The same is true for solar power. Currently, there is no obvious solution for the next big energy source that could replace oil.

Remember, the world will not run out of *energy*, but it will eventually run out of its current reserves of oil. Fossil fuels are energy from the sun stored within the Earth. Other sources of energy, also from the sun, do exist, but so far they only provide a small fraction of the world's energy needs. Most people recognize that fossil fuels cannot be our only energy source in the future.

If the world population continues to grow and consume oil at its current staggering pace, the Energy Information Administration estimates that global consumption will hit 4.7 billion gallons (17.8 billion L) per day by 2035, meaning that the energy industry will somehow have to increase its output by about 50 percent by that time. Peter Vosser, the chief executive officer of Shell, has said that "most of it will need to come from resources that haven't even been found yet." What will this mean for Earth and for human beings? Will that much oil really be needed, or will other forms of energy come into greater use? Planet Earth may not generate more petroleum in the next few decades, but its inhabitants will probably begin to live with a more diverse energy policy.

CRITICAL THINKING

- What is energy independence? Do you think it is possible, or necessary? Do you think that energy independence is an appropriate goal, or do you think it is impossible?

- Why do people disagree on how much oil is left under the Earth's surface?

- What is energy efficiency? What are some ways that society has become more (or less) energy efficient?

Glossary

barrel When referring to oil, a quantity of 42 gallons (159 liters).

Big Oil The term used to describe the oil industry, especially in the Western world, which is dominated by five or six major publicly owned companies (BP plc, Royal Dutch Shell plc, Chevron Corporation, ExxonMobil Corporation and Total SA, with ConocoPhillips Company sometimes included).

blowout An accident in which a well's safety measures fail and oil comes shooting out of the well.

brine Salt water that emerged from hand-drilled wells that people boiled off for salt.

crude oil The term for oil when it first is extracted from the ground and before it is refined; often a thick, dark-colored substance.

deepwater Water of 1,000 feet (305 meters) or deeper, in the context of offshore drilling.

fossil fuel Coal, oil, and natural gas. They are formed over millions of years from organic (previously living) material and found within the ground.

About the Author

Alison Gaines lives in Chicago, Illinois, but is originally from Vancouver, Washington. She has a degree in creative writing from Knox College and enjoys writing in a variety of genres, especially poetry and nonfiction. She enjoys traveling, playing the cello, and attending classical music concerts.